Orishas

An Introduction to African Spirituality and Yoruba Religion

Table of Contents

Introduction

The belief system of the Yoruba people, which may have originated millions of years ago in Nigeria, is regarded as one of the oldest religions in the world. It has since gained followers from all over the world, from the Caribbean to North America, and it's easy to see why. Its oral interpretations have piqued the interest of many, ranging from majestic tales of the Orishas to life-changing teachings of reincarnation. And, while it has been modified or intertwined with other world religions everywhere else, this high form of spirituality is still practiced in its original form in Africa.

This incredible form of devoutness dates back to the beginning of life and is now combined with other teachings; the wide variety of customs practiced in all of its forms can be difficult to comprehend.

However, once you understand why Yoruba people dance to their gods and wish to become one with them, everything will make sense. After all, there are several evident similarities between this African religion and Christianity, a much more widely practiced religion.

The Supreme Being, Olodumare, who helped create life on Earth by sending down his servant Oduduwa, is a pillar of this belief system. The loyal subject created patches of land in the middle of what is now known as Panthalassa, providing a home for the vast majority of living beings that inhabit this planet today. As a tribute to this act, Yoruba people all over the world live their lives in a highly spiritual way in order to be worthy of being accepted by Olodumare. The reason for this is primarily due to their level of understanding of how much our inner selves affect the laws of soul transmutation and the possibility of reincarnation. This is most likely why, in recent years, so many people in the Western World have become interested in this religion.

Moreover, there is much more to this faith than just evolving one's own spirituality. Yoruba people have been carrying on some of the most elemental traditions for centuries, from the way they enter into marriage to the customs involved in naming their children. These intriguing customs are also predicated on their belief in the cyclical journey of one's essence, as each event represents a stopping point for their souls. The devotees of this African spirituality allow the Orishas and Olodumare to guide them through the major events in their lives instead of dealing with seemingly pointless modern traditionalism. And by introducing these traditions to everyone in their circle, they ensure that everyone's soul is reborn in the next generation.

If you are just beginning to learn about African spirituality, this book can help you understand its origins and fundamental concepts. Aside from getting a glimpse into the life of the Yoruba people of Africa, you will also learn about their gods and the different Orishas. It is an excellent way to immerse yourself in this extremely detailed philosophy. So, if you are keen to learn more about spiritual life and the soul, this is a great place to start. And if you are interested in delving into the oldest theory about the origin of life, you should keep reading.

Chapter 1:

The Yoruba Culture

The Yoruba are one of Africa's most dominant ethnic groups, particularly south of the Sahara. Though the majority of Yoruba are Nigerians, members of this ethnic group are also native to Togo and Benin, among others. The Yoruba people constitute about 15.5% of the total population of the country, Nigeria.

History of the Yoruba People

The Yoruba people can be traced back to the old Ife-Ife city and the Oyo Empire between the 17th and 19th centuries. The Oyo Empire was the dominant source of military and political power for the Yoruba people. Ife-Ife retained its religious significance to the Yoruba, despite its political decline.

Ife-Ife was said to have been created by the deities Oduduwa and Obatala, the latter of whom was responsible for the creation of humans out of clay.

According to mythology, after ascending to the throne in Ife-Ife, Oduduwa had a son who would become King of the Oyo Empire.

The Oyo Empire was ruled by a king, known as Oba Alaafin. This was not a hereditary position, as it is in most European monarchies. Instead, kings were chosen by the Oyo Mesi, a group of seven councilors with legislative authority. The Oyo Mesi was governed by the Ogboni, who represented popular opinion among the citizens and were supported by religious authority due to their status as an Earth cult.

The empire was in decline by the late 1700s as a result of a political crisis that saw four successive kings on the throne in a short period of time. Following this tumultuous period, Abiodun, the king, involved the empire in a series of civil wars, hastening its eventual devastation.

Following the collapse of the Oyo Empire, the Yoruba found themselves at war with the Fulani. While the Fulani never conquered Oyo, the war resulted in the formation of independent city-states, resulting in a full-fledged civil war. This weakened them to the point where they could no longer resist colonization.

Much of historical Yorubaland (the Yoruba homeland, which includes modern-day Benin, Togo, and Nigeria) is now integrated into Nigeria. Ibadan, Lagos, Akure, and Ijebu-Ode are major Yoruba cities. Aside from a significant presence in Africa, the Yoruba have a sizable diaspora that includes recent immigrants to the United States and the United Kingdom, as well as descendants of Yoruba, abducted as slaves during the Transatlantic Slave Trade.

Yoruba Culture

Religion

Today, most Yoruba people are either Muslim or Christian. However, the traditional Yoruba religion still holds a place of importance.

Islam and Christianity

In the 14th century, the Yoruba people were introduced to Islam due to trade with Islamic merchants from the Mali Empire. Islam was adopted early in the history of Yorubaland and the Yoruba people, and many of those kidnapped as slaves and taken to the Americas were Muslims.

Christianity, on the other hand, was introduced by Europeans. The Yoruba were the first major groups in Africa introduced to it after contact with the Portuguese in the 16th century.

While Christian missions to the area were prevalent, they were relatively ineffective. The conversion of a slave boy, Samuel Crowther, in the 19th century, was the most significant catalyst for large-scale conversions. Crowther, a gifted linguist, would then use his abilities to propagate Christianity throughout Yorubaland.

Traditional Yoruba Religion

The concept of destiny, known as "ayanmo," is remarkably important in traditional Yoruba religion. People strive to achieve perfection and become one with the divine Creator by fulfilling their destiny.

In Yoruba mythology, Olorun, also known as Olodumare, is the omnipotent Creator God. Olorun sends orishas to connect the mortal and immortal worlds and protect those who worship him in order to help guide humanity.

Apart from Olorun, two other important supreme beings in Yoruba mythology are Nana Buluku (also known as a Nana Bukuu), who is either the female or androgynous version of the Supreme God, and Olofi, who is a conduit between heaven and Earth.

In some versions, Olorun and Olodumare are distinct entities. In other versions, they, along with Olofi, are regarded as three facets of the same being.

There are believed to be up to 40 orishas, depending on the source. While all of the orishas are important, Ogoun and Shango are given special attention. Ogoun is the Orisha of metalwork, and Shango is associated with fire, lightning, warriors, masculinity, and virility. He used to be an Oyo king.

Rites of Passage

There are several major rites of packages individuals must pass through during their lives.

Birth

When a child is born, he or she is often sprinkled with water to induce crying, and the Yoruba believe that no one in the vicinity of the child can speak until the child cries. Furthermore, no one under the age of the mother is permitted to be present during the birth.

The infant is taken to the backyard after birth during home births, where the umbilical cord is bound with thread and cut. The placenta is also buried, and the child is bathed and palm oil anointed over the burial site. The child is then held by the feet and shook three times, which the Yoruba believe will ensure the baby grows up strong and courageous.

Naming Customs

In Yoruba culture, naming a child is one of the most important life events. A newborn's name is carefully chosen because the Yoruba people believe that names help determine a child's destiny and that the child is meant to live out the meaning of their name.

As a result, parents conduct extensive research before settling for a name. Some families have pre-existing naming customs that can be beneficial, typically derived from a traditional familial profession or the Orisha the family worships above all others.

Children must undergo a naming ceremony, which involves significant pomp and ceremony. The actual naming is seen as gifting the child with a name, and it is a gift that comes with additional gifts, including money and clothes. It is not only the parents who name the baby, but many extended family members also give them names. This can often result in a child having over a dozen names.

There are some common "types" of names that a newborn will have, including:

- **Predestined Name:** Determined by the circumstances of a child's birth. For example, twins have predestined names depending on their birth order. The same goes for single-parent children, those born when the parents are away from home, and those born on a festival day. Other circumstances that determine a predestined name include the position a baby is born in.

- **Birth Name:** These are names given during the naming ceremony, most commonly held on the seventh day after a child's birth for girls and the ninth day after a child's birth for boys. Names are most commonly based on family tradition or significant events during (or right after) the delivery.

- **Abiku Names:** In Yoruba belief, some children are born to die. This is considered a reference to the high rates of infant mortality hundreds of years ago and the understanding that some families have higher infant mortality rates than others. Children born to such families are often given names to prevent them from dying prematurely as well, with common names including Malomo ("do not go again") and Durojaiye ("stay and enjoy life").

- **Oriki:** These are essentially pet names or praise names and refer to the child's family background or the hopes a speaker has for a child.

Marriage

While marriages are traditionally arranged; as times change, allowances have been made for romantic matches. These matches, however, must be approved by the respective parents before the couple can marry.

The wedding date is set after consulting the orishas with the assistance of a Babalawo (priest). Before this date, the groom must pay the bride's parents a bride price, which is usually paid in three installments. To avoid tragedies, the couple is forbidden from leaving their town once the date is set.

Marriage is regarded as a union of two families, not just the bride and groom, and the wedding is celebrated as lavishly as possible. The bride is escorted by her family and friends to the door of her new home, where she observes the Ekun Iyawo.

The Ekun Iyawo, which translates to "the cry of a new bride," is a ritual in which the bride weeps. This is supposed to symbolize her grief over leaving her childhood home and her parents, as well as her presence in her new home. When she enters the groom's home, her feet are washed to remove any bad luck she may have brought with her.

In one tradition, the bride is provided an igba (a calabash or a vessel shaped to resemble one) and asked to break it. She is expected to have the same number of children as the number of pieces the igba breaks into.

A woman divides her time between her marital and natal homes for the first eight days after her marriage. She does not move in fully with her new husband until the ninth day.

This traditional ceremony is often seen as a prelude to the religious ceremony or an engagement celebration by Yoruba people who are also practicing Christians or Muslims.

Funerals

Funerals, the final of the significant Yoruba rites of passage, have their own customs and rituals. Death, according to the Yoruba, is not the end of life, but a transition from one form of existence to another, which is unknown. While immortality is desired, only the ignorant fear death.

The afterlife is thought to be a continuation of life as we know it, albeit in a different location. This afterlife, however, can only be obtained if the deceased lived a moral and upright life. As a result, when a person dies well, it is regarded as a cause for celebration.

If the deceased left children or grandchildren, they would be responsible for the celebration. Even those who die young can have an afterlife, and those who die well should be celebrated regardless of their age.

Customarily, the actual burial would be performed by members of the deceased's clan. They must, however, be adult men and not close relatives. Traditionally, a grave would be dug in the same room where the deceased lived, though this is extremely uncommon nowadays. Following the burial, there would be a memorial service (celebration of life).

The Yoruba also believe that their ancestors watch over them and influence their lives. As a result, they practice ancestor veneration, in which they make an effort to remember their ancestors as frequently as possible. It is essential to understand that this is not the same as ancestor worship and should not be confused.

Yoruba Art

Art is an integral part of Yoruba life and religion, and it is thought to have originated with the creation of humans by Orisha Obatala. Obatala made the first artistic creation by sculpting humans out of clay. Indeed, a common Yoruba greeting to pregnant women is "May Obatala fashion for us a good work of art."

The Yoruba have a long artistic history and are best known for their sculptors who work in terracotta, copper, stone, bronze, and brass. One central element in Yoruba art is the Orí-Inú, the inner spiritual head.

The Orí-Inú, or inner spiritual head, is a central element in Yoruba art.

Every house has a shrine built to the Orí-Inú, with the Orí represented by a terracotta head. A person's life is determined by the Orí, and sacrifices must be made to Orí-Isese, the ruler of all Orí, to ward off evil and ensure a person enjoys good fortune and happiness.

Metalwork, which is seen to honor Ogun, the god of iron, is another popular art form. Furthermore, Yoruba culture has a masquerade tradition based on the belief that the body is merely a vessel in which the soul is held. Masquerades such as Egúngún, Gelede, and Epa all involve the creation and donning of intricate and artistic masks.

Chapter 2:

The Yoruba Beliefs

Yoruba beliefs are based on highly spiritual concepts and encompass a wide range of practices passed down through oral traditions. These customs evolved from a small ethnic group in Nigeria to a now widespread religious system through migration, merging, and the power of the human voice. Those who practice this religion believe that all human souls go through a cycle called "Ayanmo", and this determines their fate in the next life. This belief, according to the Yoruba, stems from the fact that a person can choose their own destiny - and not just in their current life. In fact, during one life, a person can decide every aspect of the future of their soul long before the spirit is reborn. Everything can be predetermined by the decisions they make in the present, from where they will live to their purpose in life to how they will die in their next life.

Although the Yoruba acknowledge that all previous plans are forgotten when the soul is reborn into a new body, they also claim that their memories can be regained during life. According to Yoruba teachings, each person's success and struggles on Earth are direct results of their attempts to remember their destiny. If they do, they may be able to claim the future they have planned ahead of time. In this quest, devotees often invoke the supreme deity, Olodumare, who lives in the skies and accepts every deserving soul. Human spirits are expected to become one with Olodumare after leaving the dying body, achieving transcendence, and living forever in a state of high bliss. Since the highest divinity is also the source of all energy, this being has limitless power to influence the path of every soul. To carry out their carefully proposed plans, each person must act and think in a way that pleases Olodumare. For the Yoruba, this entails constant spiritual development and consciously anchoring every aspect of their lives in order to be a better person. If they succeed in this quest, they will be able to prove that their soul is worthy of a place in the spiritual realm of another life.

According to Yoruba teachings, each life and death are merely minor components of a continuous cycle in which human souls occupy various forms of physical bodies in each life. Meanwhile, one's spirit gradually evolves towards eternal transcendence while living in each body and following the right path. Over time, more and more people in Ife-Ife came to value this philosophy and even took it outside of the birthplace of their civilization. As the number of followers grew, the Supreme Being was increasingly invoked. As a result, a large number of mediators have been created to facilitate communication between Olodumare and its devoted followers. These beings are known as the Orishas, and you will learn more about them later in this book.

Nowadays, a plethora of various facets of African spirituality exists under different names. Some are still practiced in their purest form in Africa, while others can be traced to the conglomeration of cultural practices brought to the New World by all Africans. Santeria is the second most widely practiced African religion after the original Yoruba religion. Santeria, which arose from a small gathering of Cuban slaves of Yoruba descent, is a hybrid of Catholicism and the original belief system. The divinities are identified with Roman Catholic saints in this form, and joining is only possible after a specific initiation period. Aside from that, nearly all of the beliefs and practices are similar to those of the original Yoruba religion. In the same way that people in Ife believed in divination, spirit possession, animal sacrifices, and initiation, so did Santeria followers. In a similar vein, enslaved Yoruba in Brazil developed their own version of African religion known as Candomble. Its practices are virtually similar to those of Yoruba, right down to how deities communicate with devotees through mediators. Candomble has saints as deities as more effort was made to preserve its African roots. Their names, however, are more accurate to the original versions and not the Catholic ones.

Creation

The elaborate tale of how life on Earth was created is one of the fascinating myths of Yoruba. According to most oral sources, the creation began when another higher being, Obatala, approached Olodumare, the ruler of the heavens, with an intriguing request. No creature could live in this world because it was completely covered by water up until that point. So, in order to change this, Obatala wished to create a few patches of dry land in the world of water, which we now call the superocean Panthalassa. With permission from the Supreme Being, Obatala began his descent from the heavens on a gold chain, carrying a bag filled with sand with snail shells mixed in it, a palm nut, a white hen, and a black cat. He spilled the sand and released the hen to spread the grains around, creating the land in the shape of valleys and mountains as the chain was long enough to reach the water. When Obatala reached the ground, he named the place he landed on "Ife" and made it his home. He planted the palm nut, which grew into a tree and produced seed, resulting in the growth of more palm trees. Obatala used palm nuts to make a variety of products, including wine, to pass the time. While sipping this intoxicating concoction, he began to carve small clay figures. Because he found it lonely to drink wine alone, he asked Olodumare to bring the clay shapes to life, thereby creating mankind. And, because he made them by hand, this explains the vast differences that exist between various human bodies. Human bodies were later endowed with Ashe, a spirit-like force that they share with all living things (including the weather and the deities).

However, not all of the other gods were pleased with the existence of mankind. Olokun, the goddess of the water world, summoned a massive wave that washed away the majority of human-built cities. Fortunately, some of the humans survived and offered a sacrifice to the Supreme Being, pleading for mercy. Olodumare listened and ended the flood by making a patch of land reappear.

Olodumare

The entire philosophy of this religion is based on a supreme being called Olodumare (also called Olorun, Oluwa, Eleda, and God). While there isn't much information about this entity, its powers and immortality have never been challenged. Furthermore, there is no centralized location where this genderless, God-like creature can be worshiped. Instead, it is celebrated in one's everyday actions as well as special celebrations held by families and communities. Olodumare is recognized as someone with the highest authority in the world. Yoruba people believe that nothing happens unless their god approves of it. Its descendants, the Orishas, share the same attributes, but they have less authority and must answer to it at all times.

Other Entities

Ancestral Spirits

The spirits of the ancestors, along with other benevolent essences, are thought to linger in this world. They keep an eye on their family members and guide them through various life challenges until they are ready to be rejuvenated. The Yoruba believe that an ancestor's spirit is reborn in a child from the same family, which explains their traditional naming practices. These ancestors are remembered and mentioned in everyday conversations in the same way they were when they were alive. Furthermore, their living relatives can communicate with them, occasionally requesting that they protect them from dangerous situations and corrupt behavior. Ancestral spirits are honored through communal celebrations as a token of gratitude for their protection.

Ajogun

Ajogun are beings who represent the negative forces of nature and can cause a variety of mishaps in one's life. These demon-like creatures can be blamed for everything, from accidents to illnesses to social problems. Almost every danger, illness, or mishap-afflicted person is either bewitched or possessed by an evil spirit, according to Yoruba traditional religion. To be cured, they must go to a priest for divination rituals and, if possible, advice on how to get rid of whatever is bothering them.

Ashe

Humans, natural elements, Orishas, and deities all possess Ashe as an inner force. This power, if attained, can determine one's fate by occasionally pushing them in the direction of good or bad. When contained in natural elements such as lightning, rain, wind, or even blood, the Supreme Being completely determines its character. In humans, however, it can be influenced, and this can begin as early as birth by giving a child a specific name.

Yoruba Spiritual Practices

Some of the practices of African spirituality have drastically changed as it has spread rapidly and merged with other religions. A few devotees, however, continue to practice their ancestors' traditional religion. These include honoring the gods and the

Orishas in everyday life as well as participating in special celebrations. During these festivals, sacrifices are made to the various gods in order to ask them to favorably influence things like rain, temperature, and sunshine and provide a plentiful harvest for mankind to survive. Aside from that, entire Yoruba religious festivals are devoted to the ritualistic re-enactment of their old legends and mythical tales, which help explain mankind's place in the universe.

The most common reasons for Yoruba religious festivals are to commemorate births, marriages, and the dead. Initiations and other rites of passage are also common in Yoruba culture. The Yoruba pay homage to their ancestors in both body and spirit by taking part in these ceremonies. In these times, entire family lines are celebrated by expressing the spiritual beliefs of the living as well as their ancestors. The way they express their own spiritual beliefs, from their traditional dresses to the music they dance to, is highly valued. These religious traditions also serve a socially beneficial purpose. After all, they were created in part to promote spiritual connections throughout the community by encouraging families to help one another.

When it comes to Yoruba celebrations honoring higher beings, one of the most important rituals takes place during the traditional yam harvest. A sacrifice is made in honor of Ifa, the deity of wisdom and hard work, and the new yam is cut, followed by a feast, music, and dancing. Prayers are also said at the end of each year to ward off premature deaths and to ask Olodumare and the Orishas for protection for the entire village in the coming year. To prove their worthiness to Ogun, priests take a vow to remain celibate, abstain from fighting, and even refrain from eating certain foods during the annual festival of Ogun. By offering palm oil, kola nuts, snails, and even animal sacrifices, the Yoruba appease Ogun and entice him to join their cause rather than destroy it.

Reincarnation

Yoruba spirituality emphasizes the role of a higher spirit in reincarnation, in addition to having a productive and generous existence for achieving personal goals in this life. According to its teachings, being a good person is necessary if one wants their soul to be reborn. Most followers hope to earn the privilege of reincarnation, they will strive to be helpful and kind people. They know that the souls of unkind and deceitful persons will be denied transmutation and won't get the chance to come back in the next generation. The spirits who come back are reborn in the bodies of the children born in the same families. This concept of familial reincarnation is known as Atunwa - and is the main reason why Yoruba children at birth often get several names belonging to their ancestors. It's believed that when a child is born, they carry all their ancestors' wisdom in their soul. The naming tradition is helping their soul find all this accumulated knowledge during their lifetime.

Chapter 3:

The Orishas

The Orishas were Yoruba deities who spread across Nigeria and other Western African regions a few centuries ago. Over time, a large portion of their population that established their base on the West African coast adopted their religious beliefs. The ambiguity surrounding Orisha persists due to their intervening nature and peculiar characteristics.

Who Are the Orishas?

In essence, an Orisha was a supernatural entity or deity associated with the tribes of southwestern Nigeria, particularly the Yoruba. However, beliefs and powers related to the Orishas spread steadily across the southeastern parts of the region, which the Edo people kept track of. In addition to these two tribes, the Fon of Benin and the Ewe of Ghana and Togo started to believe in the Orishas. While the Yoruba referred to their deities as Orishas, the other tribes referred to them as "voduns." Despite the fact that each tribe has its own version of the myth and rituals, the religious concept and emanation of the beliefs remain the same.

For better understanding, several records claim the Orishas to be deities of the Western African people. However, a lot of debate surrounding the actual form of the Orishas has supervened to date. While some argue that an Orisha was actually a supernatural entity that defines the anthropomorphic silhouette of a god or a deity, some believe them to be a supreme being branched out of god's supremacy who could be a defied ancestor or a powerful force aligning and converging objects in the right place. They are neither god nor humans but a powerful force that links to the multidimensional universe and binds objects, creatures, and powers to each other. They are also commonly referred to as "orisa" or "orixa."

The Creator of the universe, Olorun (also called Eledumare or Olodumare), commissioned a group of agents, the Orishas. This group of powerful spirits was linked to primordial energies that could create or destroy every entity within the cosmos. They are the trough through which everything and everyone was born and started existing in the world. In other words, they acted as mediators between supernatural powers and living beings. Just like the powers of the Creator cannot be measured, the Orishas can also not be counted as they exist in innumerable figures. They are believed to be descended from Orun, the Orisha of the sky/heaven, and have been governing the manifestations of the universe ever since.

According to a popular legend associated with the Odu Oshe Otura, a group of primordial gods or irunmoles were sent into the universe to bring life to the world they were creating. Before the creation, Olodumare bestowed supreme power on the seventeen deities. The only woman in the group, Oshun, was ignored by the other sixteen irunmoles, which gradually hampered the process. The other deities were unaware of Oshun's power and significance in the creation of the universe. For conventional creation, a proper balance of male and female energies was required. The creation process was halted due to a lack of participation on both sides.

With the absence of Oshun, the process transpired into chaos, which is when the other deities summoned Oshun to continue working with them. Initially, she refused, as the exclusion hurt her pride. However, as the other gods begged her to return and asked for her forgiveness, Oshun released her grudge and rejoined the forces. After they created the world, the irunmoles headed to the mortal realm and settled there for a while. They took part in battles, completed several feats, died, and returned to the world after being reincarnated into other beings. The Yoruba tribe believed them to be immortal spirits capable of both destruction and creation, and worshipped them as deities.

Over time, the significance of these spirits spread across the region and even reached the Western world. The Orishas were worshipped across the world, with devotees hailing from the United States, Brazil, Trinidad, and Cuba. Among the Orishas, Oya, Shango, Oshun, Yemoja, and Ogun were the principal deities involved in the creation process. Yemoja represents all the rivers and salty water bodies and signified motherhood, while Shango represents thunder, smoke, and fire.

Ogun represents war and iron, Oya repres destructive nature of winds, and Oshun represents femininity and fertility.

The Orishas died and reincarnated after centuries of suffering, tragedy, and destruction in the world. The deities' new form drew several parallels between their ancient and altered embodiments. Since the Orishas endured a number of changes at the crux, worshipping them became a tough challenge for the Yoruba people. They had to sacrifice themselves to please the Orishas. In fact, this act became a deeply ingrained belief in the Yoruba religion.

According to the Yoruba people, 400 + 1 orishas exist, the +1 signifying infinity and the idea of innumerable deities. Basically, you can think of as many deities as you like or believe in. However, you must add another number to express the existence of innumerable gods. Some records state that around 400 to 700 Orishas existed in the past. Others claim the number to be 1,440. Due to this ambiguity, the Orishas as mainly perceived as a group of gods with countless members.

Primarily, the Orishas were classified on the basis of the colors they represented, which were white and red or black. The gods representing the white shade were believed to be gentle and cool, which is why they were called tutu. On the other hand, the assertive, strong, and bold gods were called gbig-bona and conformed to the black and red shades that essentially depict a heaviness. Every deity favored a particular object, food, and color that helped them stand apart and developed distinctive characteristics.

While some Orishas were saved during the Trans-Atlantic Slave Trade, the others were lost midway. Some were even adapted as different versions to fit the beliefs. Despite the cultural and religious differences, the Orishas were perceived as supernatural entities that governed human existence and the nature of the cosmos. The people across the world conjointly called them "Saints" or "Santos." The Orishas were divine spirits but still represented human-like traits, which made them god's mediators. These traits helped shape the beliefs and induced the base for a distinct religion.

Despite their mystical nature, human beings could relate to the Orishas' flaws and mistakes, which strengthened their beliefs and increased their respect. They were able to relate to the deities and worshiped them in order to get closer to God. They were the only ones who could truly liberate the people and lead them in the right direction.

The Concept of Orishas

The word "Orisha" comes from the part, "ori" meaning head or the top physical anatomical part of a creature in the Yoruba language. The main head or ori is not just one's physical head but also a channel or a vessel to the internal head, ori-inu, or internal ori. "Orisha" literally translates to "selected heads" or "special heads." The Yoruba people also referred to them as sages or "dema deities." A person's internal head is the representation of their personality, thoughts, character, and spirit. The ori-inu is unique for every being and is gifted by god. It determines the person's fate and controls their actions. Even though a minor part of the person's changed mindset and actions can impact their fate, a major part of their journey is written beforehand. This is extensively determined by their ori-inu.

The ori-inu follows a set of rules that can shift according to the manifestation of one's actions. The ile ori, or the head's house, acts as a witness for the ori-inu and is shaped like a shrine resembling a crown and adorned with cowrie shells. The crown can be deemed the soul's container that represents a person's fortune. The cowrie shells represent the person's social status, opportunities, and wealth. It is believed that the ile ori can also represent the additional prayers and shrines included inside the structure to guide the person in the right direction. The cowrie shells are white in color and depict purity and a noble character.

In the past, cowrie shells were used for trading goods and exchanging rare items. This form of currency and economic symbol added the significance of wealth and monetary status to the shells. Furthermore, the shells are also intricately linked to eiye ororo, a white-feathered bird representing a person's mind. The entire concept of ile ori signifies the importance of having a good character, a noble personality, and a generous heart, which collectively epitomizes true wealth.

This hierarchy begins at the head and works its way down to the toe. It is also used to describe the Yoruba people's social status and way of life. A person's character and stature are determined by their head, this metaphor has become ingrained in society. The community's leader was figuratively the people's "head," giving them an advantage. They were highly regarded due to their influence and rank. Along with rank and status, the age of others was a significant factor in determining a person's status. Over time, this resulted in the establishment of a society-wide hierarchy that everyone was obliged to follow.

Chapter 4:

Types of Orishas

In general, the Orishas can be distinguished based on their gender and favored color or food. However, some records depict a profound classification of the deities to trace a pattern and strengthen the beliefs of the Yoruba people. This also helps us understand the myths of the world's creation and illustrate a rugged timeline of how things came into being.

Olodumare, the Creator of the cosmos, was the supreme god and head of the Orishas. Olodumare was thought to have no gender and was assigned all tasks related to the creation of the world without actively participating in it. The Yoruba people were supposed to pay more recognition to the Orishas.

Classification of Orishas

The Orishas can be classified into three groups- primordial deities (the ones present before and during the creation of the world), the defied ancestors (the ones that stayed in the world after its creation), and personified natural forces (natural elements of the world). Among all Orishas, only five to six were considered the most influential, which are placed in these categories based on their traits and knowledge of existence. The basis of this classification is not rigid and can be retraced to mark the instances that overlap.

Primordial Divinities

The deities or spiritual energies that existed before the creation of the world and human beings were known as primordial divinities or deities in the Yoruba religion. They descended from the Creator of the universe and were known as the agents employed by the god. This is mainly why they are known as the "people of heaven" or "ara orun." They did not need help from humans to transcend into the world. With the blessings and powers showered by the supreme god, the primordial divinities breathed life into the world. It is believed that after the creation of the world, the primordial deities headed back to heaven and continue to reside with the supreme god.

Eshu Elegbara

Eshu Elegbara, known for his vices and tricks, is a messenger who carries information from the Earth to heaven and vice versa. In essence, he serves Ifa, the chief god, who relies on Eshu (as he is commonly known) for updates. Eshu is in charge of all life transitions, and he frequently seeks conciliation in the form of sacrifice (main tobacco) and divine information. He also guards Ifa and protects the crossroads. However, as the trickster god, Eshu is constantly pranking the other Orishas and the chief god. According to legend, Eshu tricked Ifa into divulging the secrets of sanctity and divinity.

Eshu was extremely relevant and significant to the Yoruba religion. Unlike other Orishas who had dedicated days for worship, Eshu was worshipped for most days of the week. In fact, the believers hesitated to pray to the upper gods without seeking permission from Eshu as he was the closest agent of the chief god. Since Eshu was responsible for every person's fate and life journey, a minor mishap or change in your path could be a signal from the irunmole. The changes could be either minimal or entirely transform one's life.

While Eshu Elegbara was widely believed to be the same god, some accounts distinguish them as brothers. Elegbara was responsible for his worshippers' fate and life direction, whereas Eshu was the trickster god who indulged in pranks. This Orisha represented and governed people's lives from the moment they leave their homes until they return safely. Eshu scrutinized any minor or major change when outside. In other words, Eshu depicted the concept of chance, which was a powerful symbolization. Even though not many favor chances and changes due to the lack of comfort and satisfaction, the Orisha ameliorated their fears by conveying that the changes would lead to something better and more uplifting over time.

Paths of Eshu: Some of the notable paths or avatars of Eshu Elegbara include Eshu Alaroye/Laroye, Eshu Bi, Eshu Alagwanna/Lagwanna, Eshu Aina/BaraAina, Eshu Anaki, Eshu Arerebioko, Eshu Alaketu, Eshu Aye, Eshu Ashikuelu, Eshu Ana, Eshu Afra, Eshu Alboni, Eshu Dako, Eshu Bara Layiki, Eshu Ayeru, Eshu Owo, Eshu Beleke, Eshu Ode/Ode Mata, and Eshu Eluufe. Even though all these avatars of Eshu possess distinct characteristics, they collectively represent an Orisha who supervised the fates of people.

Obatala

The deity of life and creation of humans, Obatala is worshipped due to his ability to bring and shape life. He shapes babies when they are still in their mother's womb. Commonly known as the Sky Father, the irunmole's symbol is a white dove. White snails and elephants are also believed to his animal spirits. Obatala is believed to possess the ownership of all heads until the person seeks priesthood under a particular Orisha. Since the heads are the shrine of souls, Obatala governed his worshippers' heads and souls. The color white is closely linked to Obatala as it depicts purity, wisdom, and clarity. This Orisha was well-known for his wisdom and ability to make powerful decisions. The other deities also respected him as they believed judgment and clarity to precede confusion and disagreement.

Obatala's wife was the mother goddess, Yemaya, and both collectively ruled Ife, the first Yoruba city. According to this account, he is a deified ancestor, the second classification of the Orishas.

However, the myth claims him to be a primordial deity because he was thought to be a descendant of the chief god. Obatala is known to be the oldest of all primordial deities. After the cosmos' Creator acknowledged his wisdom and clarity, he was given the task of creating humans. However, Obatala's liking towards Plan Wine mellowed his thinking capacity and dulled his clear mind. Over time, he started creating humans with disabilities such as blindness, deafness, and other issues.

However, some records state that these actions were necessary and imperfect humans needed evolution to occur. He offered help by protecting the disabled and ensuring peace and serenity in their lives. Obatala is also responsible for healing people, and his gentle demeanor gave him the name of a "level-headed" Orisha. He is patient, calm, and listens to both sides of the story to bring justice. However, he always has a slight inclination towards those who can control their feelings and emotions. The Yoruba people offered water, sugar, milk, white flowers, and white rice to Obatala to keep him happy.

Paths of Obatala: Alaguema, Ocha Griñan, Ayagunna, Oba Lofun, Oba Moro, Yeku Yeku,

Baba Acho, Orisha Aye, Obanla, Osanla, Osalufon, Ochanla, Oshalufon, Oshanla, and Ochalufon.

Orunmila

The deity of knowledge and wisdom, Orunmila represents a person's fate and prophecy. Along with Obatala, Orunmila was also extremely curious about the human form, which led him to study the facets of human creation and breathing life into them. He represents purity and is considered important as he was present during the creation of the world. Orunmila was given the second-highest rank among all agents, which gave him the name "Igbakeji Olodumare." Ifa, the chief god, entered the world with the help of Orunmila. He symbolizes fate, wisdom, and omniscience that gave him a significant stance among other Orishas. His name translates to "heaven aware of our salvation."

Orunmila is also known as "Eleri Ipin," the witness of destiny and creation. He helps individuals transform their perspectives by teaching valuable lessons. Orunmila is the symbol of greatness. He inspires his worshippers to be as wise as him and thrive to achieve the honor that all Orishas possess.

If you follow the path of sanity and perform noble deeds without expecting results, you will steadily rise to greatness and transcend to the other realm. Orunmila narrates the tales and experiences mentioned in Odu Ifa, a file representing life events from the present and the past. From notable victories to ancestors' trails, every minor to major detail is entailed in several files of Odu Ifa.

Furthermore, Orunmila is also assigned the task of decoding these past and present life experiences to shape an eventful future. He manages to decipher the events that will likely take place and mold it for a favorable outcome. He uses his wisdom and extracts the best pieces from the past and merges them with the present. During the creation process, Orunmila lived on Earth for around 400 years and survived by breathing in air. He traveled back and forth to heaven and Earth to comply with the chief god's orders. After he returned to heaven, he was sent back to shape humans.

Defied Ancestors

The supreme ancestors of humans who held high ranks and supervised others were believed to be the Orishas who took a new form to exist in the newly created world. They existed as great rulers, heads of significant communities, heroes, founders of new communities and cities, warriors, and other respected individuals. They held a superior position and were recognized by all. The defied ancestors influenced others around them and inspired young humans to aim higher. They also had the ability to mold the force of natural elements to their favor and redirect their destructive power towards the enemies.

The defied ancestors made numerous sacrifices and offerings to the chief god in order to achieve and strengthen this power of control. When the time came for them to leave the world, they either vanished without a trace or vanished in spectacular ways, such as turning into a rock, rising to the skies, or plummeting into the ground. Such occurrences marked the transformation of the defied ancestors into true Orishas, which they were destined to undergo at the appropriate time. Today, the descendants of the defied ancestors are actively promoting their cause.

Shango

Shango is the deity of lightning and thunder. He ruled the kingdom of Oyo and symbolized male sexuality, fertility, virility, music, sky, and justice. He is represented by the colors white and red, which depict a mixture of purity, enticement, and passion. Shango is believed to be close to Oshun, Oba, and Oya and often gets intimate with them. He dislikes Ogun, and both prefer to keep a distance from each other. The worshippers of Shango are true devotees as the deity protects them from bad energies and keeps them away from evil eyes. The Yoruba people offered mugwort, copper, red palm oil, spicy foods, sugar, and red wine or rum to Shango to keep him happy.

Shango carries a powerful ax that is symbolic of his image. Among all Orishas, he was the most powerful, which is also why the other deities feared him. His wisdom and strength gave the kingdom of Oyo one of the most deserving and powerful rulers of all time. Despite his short rule of only seven years, he made significant changes to his kingdom that impacted its aftermath. The region grew exponentially until one day, Shango's palace was destroyed by lighting. During the 19th century, the kingdom of Oyo led a revolt against the Afonja but eventually collapsed.

Following the defeat of the Oya Empire, some Yoruba people were sent to the Western part of the world and assigned as slaves. They did not, however, forget the sacrifices made by the great ruler, Shango, who was thought to be superhuman or a descendant of the Orisha. They spread Shango's beliefs throughout the world, giving rise to Shango's devotees all over the world. Ojo Jakuta is the fifth day of the week, and it is dedicated to the worship of Shango.

Paths of Shango: Shango Bumí, Shango Obadimeyi, Shango Alafin or Alafi Alafi, Shango Dibeyi, Shango Kamúkan, Shango Yakutá, Shango Olosé, Shango Obbará, Shango Bangboshé, Shango Lubbe or Bara Lubbe, Shango Obayá, Shango Olufina Kake, Shango Obaluekun, Shango Eyee, Shango Addima Addima, Shango Oloké, and Shango Yumi Kasiero, among many others.

Personified Natural Forces

All the natural elements of the world - water bodies, trees, earth, wind, and mountains were believed to be possessed by supreme spirits that helped the humans in some way. The Yoruba worshipped the Orishas on-site, where they supposedly existed within the natural entities. Religious beliefs held power to control the movement of the natural forces if the rituals were performed in a certain way. However, the natural forces could not be explored to their core, which gave them their wild character as we know of today. The ability to tame the forces and the existence of the deified ancestors were intricately linked. The Orishas' altar, which coerced their powers and became a significant part of the deities, was also said to be one of the witnessing objects.

Yemaya

The Water Goddess, Yemaya, is worshiped as the spirit of the oceans and water bodies representing growth and fertility. She symbolizes motherhood and is known to attract several gods due to her sexuality. The Orisha of rivers, Oshun, is Yemaya's brother, and both collectively govern the world's water bodies. Yemaya can be extremely calm and giving to humans and living creatures, but she can also get angry and destructive in nature. When she is happy and calm, she gives abundant food and possessions to humans. However, if she is angered, she can bring floods and natural calamities to destroy their livelihoods.

Yemaya and Oya are rivals and are never seen together. While Yemaya protects all humans from their shortcomings, she is particularly more concerned about women and children. Those who are neglected or abandoned can pursue Yemaya for protection. She also has a special place for travelers who often need to cross seas and oceans to reach the other side. Individuals born under the water sign are closely associated with Yemaya and her powers. Several myths depict Yemaya as a mermaid who is adorned with a beautiful outfit made of crystals, shells, and corals. The Yoruba people offered jewelry, perfumes, seashells, watermelon, coral, lamb, duck, flowers, pomegranate, coconut cake, plantain chips, and molasses to Yemaya to keep her happy.

Due to the various images and manifestations of Yemaya found around the world, she is regarded as having a hampered consciousness by various religions. She is a powerful and virtual natural force that nourishes and protects humans as a whole. Yemaya is associated with the numbers ten and seven. Yemaya not only provides nourishment and protection, but she also aids in the healing of emotional distress. She inspires people to love and accept themselves as they are and to set healthy boundaries. However, if she discovers anyone crossing her domain or disrespecting her turf, she has the power to turn the tides and order destruction. She can be both fierce and intimidating, as well as calm and patient.

Paths of Yemaya: Yemaya Oquette (similar to Kali Ma of Hindu mythology), Yemaya Oggun Ayipo (protector of the elderly), Yemaya Ibu Akinomi (destroyer), Yemaya Asseu (lives in polluted waters), Yemaya Ita Tanan (warrior with a sword), Yemaya Okuti (ruler of the witches), Yemaya Ibu Okoto (the one who resides within shells), Yemonja Banyarin (protector of children), Yemaya Ibu Ina (queen of arguments), and Yemaya Ibubunle (sediment of water bodies and oceans), among many others.

Oshun

The deity of waters and rivers, Oshun is the symbol of fertility and growth. The Western world recognizes her as "the Orisha of love" because she represents femininity and divinity. During her existence in the world, she served as Shango's companion, which made her the queen of the kingdom of Oyo. Oshun is pure and gentle and protects those who call out to her. However, just like Yemaya, she can be equally intimidating and destructive if disrespected. The Yoruba people offered marigolds, makeup, perfumes, flowers, chamomile tea, mirror, brushes, rosemary, sandalwood, fans, honey, spinach, cinnamon, corals, and amber to Oshun to keep her happy.

These sacrifices are thought to cleanse her soul and purify her intentions, which is beneficial to humans and their fate in the long run. Oshun is associated with fertility and reproductive health, which is why she has a large female following. Some stories claim that Yemeya and Oshun are the same Orisha deity, while others claim that they are sisters. Oshun is known to be present at every successful event to bestow her blessings, but she remains hidden. Her omnipotent and omnipresent stance is, therefore, significant among the Yoruba people. Oshun spreads the importance of water as a natural force in the world. She wants people to believe that water is the greatest asset and no one is truly an enemy of this natural force.

Oshun was the only female Orisha in a group of seventeen deities who played a significant role in the creation of the world. As previously stated, her absence caused chaos, and the male gods pleaded with her to rejoin the force. The world was created as planned after she rejoined, and the balance between both energies was restored. Some cultures call Oshun by the name "Yeye," meaning "the great mother." Over time, Oshun gave birth to the trickster god and messenger of heaven and Earth, Elegba. Oshun is quick in answering prayers, which made her a famous goddess among several tribes. She believes that the world can be more beautiful if the vices and evil spirits within humans and living creatures die.

Paths of Oshun: Among several paths of Oshun, the most popular ones include Oshun Ololodí or Olodí, Oshún Ibu Yumu, Oshún Ibu Iñani or Añani, Oshún Ibu Okuanda, Oshún Ibu Oddonki, Oshún Ibu Okuase or Akuase Oddo, Oshún Ibu Itumu, Oshún Ibu Odoko, Oshún Eleke Oñí,

Oshun Gumí, Bomó or Bumí, Oshún Idere Lekun, and Oshún Aremu Kondiano.

Even though these six Orishas were considered the most influential spirits among all, others also held a significant stature. These included Ala - the Mother Goddess or Goddess of Earth, Nana Buluku - the Mother of all Mothers (the Supreme Goddess), Aja - the Forest and Animal Goddess, Erinle - the God of Medicine, Ayao - the God of Air, Kokou - the Warrior, Aganju - the God of Wilderness and Volcanoes, Sopona - the God of Smallpox, and Oxossi - the God of the Forest. Collectively, these gods ruled over the sky and governed the fate of humans. They answered prayers and healed the ones who suffered from internal and external injuries. In other words, the Orishas ensured the well-being of all living creatures.

Chapter 5:

Orishas: The Past and the Modern World

Orishas have unquestionably shaped the history of the ancient Yoruba tribes in Africa. Only a few of their original practices have survived amongst these localized groups. However, younger and modified forms of Yoruba spirituality thrived, and they did so in a variety of locations around the world. The newer branches, particularly Santeria, are gaining popularity in Western society by the day, and for good reason. In fact, the African spiritual practices have been proven to have a soothing effect on people's souls in these modern yet confusing times. Because as our technology advances, we often forget about the importance of old customs and the respect for our community. African spirituality, from what we know, has always aimed to bring people together in spirit and mind. The possibility of rebirth can also encourage you to consider what kind of person you want to be in this life and the next.

How Orishas were Utilized in the Past

There are few reliable testaments of the indigenous Yoruba's ancient ways of communicating with Orishas because they pass down their traditions through oral and practical means. In fact, the majority of the written records left behind were drafted by British colonial leaders who did not accept African spirituality as an official religion and had no interest in learning more about their customs. Fortunately, some of the most important evidence of Yoruba faith was preserved in wood carvings and woven garments. These beautiful structures, enriched with traditional elements, can give us an insight into how Orishas were used in the past, in addition to the tales and myths we are familiar with. This is also fascinating to see because these indigenous devotees are dedicated to preserving their heritage. In Africa, old traditions, such as communicating with spirits and higher beings, are still practiced in the same way. They still employ the same tools and techniques to summon an Orisha, and they do so for the same reasons they have for centuries.

The woven crowns of the Ifa kings reveal that their first ruler was a descendant of Olodumare. We can also deduce from the symbol of the bird atop it that this king was the first messenger to relay mankind's petitions to the Supreme Being. The fact that his successors wore crowns similar to his indicates that the tradition was carried on. The remaining rulers were also among the first spiritual leaders, and their spirits were revered.

A very distinctive occasion for Yoruba to consult with an Orisha was the birth of twins in the family. Despite having an extremely high rate of twin births, these children are considered a special blessing was given by the Creator. If one or both of the twins died, their essence would still be taken care of. According to Yoruba myths, the dead twin's soul remained on Earth and watched over the family. For this reason, a person appointed by Orishas had to carve out a wooden memorial image of the twins, which was cared for almost as if it was a real child.

When the Yoruba asked Eshu to mediate a conflict between two tribes, he did so with a two-faced wooden dance staff at a festival filled with music, dancing, and plenty of food. Divination from Eshu meant an infinite solution to any conflict because this Orisha can communicate with the Creator. At the same time, Eshu was appeased with a sacrifice for him not to turn on people with his malicious tricks.

As their civilization grew in Ifa and priesthood was introduced, Yoruba practitioners could now use these spiritual counselors to communicate with the Orishas. If a devotee wanted to learn an aspect of their fate, they needed to ask a priest to connect them with Orunmila. The priest used an intricately carved divination tapper to hit a diviner tray or a wooden board, and the sound would get the attention of Orunmila. This Orisha is considered the ruler of fate and often provides the petitioner with answers to their questions and guidance in life.

Contemporary Practices and Influence

Despite going through some significant changes in itself, African religion also made its own mark on other cultures. One of the most impactful ways this spirituality affects Western civilization is via the

Yoruba healing system. It's a dynamic system that uses herbal medications to cure ailments - and at the same time, the herbalists and the relatives ask the Orishas for help and divination about the fate of the ill. Apart from communicating with Orishas, each herbalist is blessed by their ancestors' knowledge and experience, accumulated over years of practice. Because of that, they can uncover and successfully heal diseases much faster and sometimes even more efficiently than Western medicine. For example, mental illnesses often remain undetected by modern diagnostic techniques until later stages. Even when these conditions are finally noted, artificial medications can't cure most of them. Additionally, physical symptoms of an illness may hide troubles with one spirit - and until those are healed, the symptoms will remain. Using their knowledge of the spiritual world, herbalists can pry into the metaphysical reasons behind an ailment and correct the person's spiritual anomaly.

In combination with Western medicine, the Yoruba healing system can be a much more efficient way to treat ailments of physical nature as well. Even some of the most serious - and unfortunately still very common - illnesses on the African continent can be treated or cured using the elemental part of the medicine. Most of these elements are easy to find in the wilderness or markets in Africa, but the African diaspora doesn't have these options. Fortunately, with modern technology, these elements can be made even more accessible and convenient to use. Herbalists in western cities can obtain traditional medicine more easily and can help more people.

Having an altar in modern Yoruba homes is quite a usual practice. Devotees of African religions don't have a temple or shrine to go for divinations or sacrifice. On special occasions, whole families gather around the altar in one home and use it for their queries or honor their Orishas in front of it. This brings people together and helps them reconnect and forge stronger spiritual bonds within the family. Apart from this, altars can be put up for several different reasons and decorated in various ways. Some have a large shrine that takes up half of a room, and they decorate it lavishly with flowers and personal belongings. Others only have room for a pocket-sized one they use to say a quick prayer. In any case, Yoruba people must construct their shrines in accordance with their convictions taking into account their own spirituality. It's not uncommon for one's altar to grow in size as their belief in the spiritual realm and trust in Orisha divinations grows. Those who do not have enough space for large religious displays keep small statues of the most powerful Orishas in their homes, one in each room.

Offering small blood sacrifices is still common, though it is practiced more frequently among indigenous groups. These rituals are usually followed by feasts and music in order to obtain an Orisha's blessing for the workers. While contemporary practitioners in the Western World also use divinations to get to their everyday lives in a spiritually sound way, they do so using different techniques. Burning incense, candles, and making traditional brews in a cauldron or pot could be just as effective to appease the higher beings. Typically, on the first day of the week, an offering should be offered to Elegua. He will help open up the spirit world, so it's recommended to begin the week by summoning him. By facilitating communication with other deities and spirits, Elegua will make it easier to interpret any divinations they provide during the rest of the week. As the week progresses, the other six most influential Orishas can be consulted for different issues. Although there isn't a specific day of the week to summon any of the Orishas, devoted practitioners feel which deity is needed in each circumstance. Through their own essence, they are able to open up to the spirit or Orisha they need the most, so they will be more ready to take on the advice or resolution they receive.

Of course, when one is offering a blood tribute for a specific purpose, this ritual could be done on any day of the week. There might be certain times of the year allocated for these purposes, but this is not uniform throughout the African religion. Different groups living in various areas have different dates which they believe to be the best. These times can be changed only if respected members of the community feel the need to modify them. At the end of the year, Olodumare is honored by a blood sacrifice for its role in the life of the Yoruba. Eshu, the trickster deity, is offered one around harvest time to keep him from impeding the workers' efforts. As these are said to be beings that possess an immense amount of power, they can be summoned at any time.

The Cultural and Social Impact of Orishas

Santeria, the Cuban branch of African spirituality developed out of necessity during the transatlantic slave trades, has since gained thousands of devotees in this country. After the devotees of Santeria started their migrations to North America, their religion quickly began to grow. Santeria devotees brought their own traditions for celebrating special occasions - along with their rituals of reaching for divinations from the Orishas. While these customs were initially frowned upon, Americans soon realized how crucial these spiritual traditions are for holding a community together. Whenever there is a dispute or trouble with the Santeria community, help or advice from an Orisha could solve it easily. If someone from one family is ill or injured, an herbalist from another one is always ready to help. And in times of great need, other material possessions are often exchanged within a community.

These communities also aim to resolve issues efficiently with outsiders, so everyone can continue to coexist peacefully.

When it comes to younger generations, they definitely emphasize the importance of outside values. They adapted some new cultural norms that are shaped by the social context surrounding them. Whereas the traditional wardrobe in old religion included colorful garments, contemporary Santerians need to wear white clothes for at least a year. This symbolizes the cleaning of their souls and is primarily used to distinguish them from other religions. Incidentally, this wear also created a fashion trend that even non-religious youngsters follow readily. Using modern audiovisual technology, followers were able to make recordings and modern soundtracks of traditional Yoruba music. With its unique rhythm combined with popular pop music, the sound of African drums has reached and touched millions of lives worldwide. When celebrated modern artists have also begun to depict Orishas in their work, this made even more people curious and open to learning more about African spirituality.

How Orishas Can Be Used in Modern Times

The traditions of African spirituality have suffered a significant setback with the technological advancement in modern societies. Rather than uniting us, digital technology appears to be dividing us even more. It takes away time that could be spent strengthening bonds within our families and creates a barrier between us and other cultures. People may feel free to express their desires and worldviews through technology, but the real world is the polar opposite. As a result, our souls suffer more and more, putting us further back on our path to personal growth.

However, as recent events proved, there has never been a greater need for making spiritual connections than in these times. The African diaspora in many countries is still subjected to discrimination - and this isn't just because of their distinct religion. If we also add all the chaos the global pandemic created to this already disorderly world, it becomes clear how much people need healing. Finding solace in one's inner strength is essential for our survival - in body and mind. By cleaning one's soul and seeking counsel from a diviner, it's much easier to deal with all the anxiety and fear that recently ensued. Even if one is only dealing with the stress of everyday life and running from one errand to another can be challenging in itself. In these times, taking just a couple of minutes a day for some self-reflection can help the soul strengthen so that we can face the challenges. By taking this time to connect with the inner spirit and then with Orishas, it's much easier to understand the situation more clearly. Immersing in Yoruba practices and using the guidance of deities is also an excellent way to connect people. This way, individual members of the same religious community can help each other's souls heal, which will help strengthen the whole community.

For all the reasons stated above, more and more people from the African diaspora are turning back to their roots. In it, they find a method to deal with the mental and emotional challenges of the modern world. The elemental religion and its Latin American variants are equally used for this purpose - as they all differ from the western norms. All these branches of African spirituality have the unique trait to offer a different way of mental healing - the one that comes from within. Additionally, instead of stressing independence, using Orishas as a community can help clean one's soul more efficiently than any other method. A practitioner often has one Orisha they feel more connected to and can rely on when needed. Being connected closely with an Orisha can be a huge advantage, as they can provide guidance in day-to-day lives. However, using the whole community to summon a spirit or a higher being can give everyone a lot more solace and clarity when it comes to the future. After all, one can only achieve the final transcendence if they are at peace with their surroundings during their lives.

The same way African slaves once used their spirituality to have brief moments of freedom during colonization and slave trades, contemporary Yoruba practitioners can tap into their religion to liberate themselves from this oppressing world driven by modern technology. In fact, everyone involved in the world of African spirituality can only gain advantages on it. Regardless of the reasons for joining and experiencing this religion, as long as one is respectful to the spiritual world and open to working within a community, one can achieve their ultimate goal. The first step is finding the inner power, beginning to grow it, and after that, everything becomes easier to handle. Furthermore, whether one is seeking answers, mentorship, or a solution to a problem, being able to rely on Orishas can be a very empowering experience.

Conclusion

From the preceding chapters of this book, you have gained a deep understanding of the fascinating history of the Yoruba. You have learned about their ancient and modern customs, as well as their myths and beliefs. Their fascinating tales are an incredible blend of their own indigenous beliefs and rich cultural traditions that have been passed down through generations. Modern African spirituality includes elements influenced by various social contexts shaped by their surroundings over centuries of existence.

According to traditional Yoruba beliefs, the soul of every person has a preordained destiny or fate, which through a series of reincarnations, finally culminates in reuniting with Olodumare, the divine Creator. As per the teaching of Yoruba, the life and the death of each person are parts of an ongoing cycle until they reach the state of final transcendence. Because the souls exist in various bodies throughout these cycles, a person's ultimate goal has to be to live each life trying to achieve this higher state. This philosophy is so important to the Yoruba ethnic group that they choose to preserve it both in Ile-Ife (the birthplace of their civilization) and wherever they have migrated as well. In its journey, this knowledge has survived everything, from slavery to the challenges of adapting to the modern world.

You have also discovered that the Yoruba have a number of intricate and colorful celebratory traditions, some of which can be observed during special family events. Their children are given one name from all of their living relatives at birth, and a child may be named after a recently deceased relative because it is believed that the ancestral spirit is reborn within them. The institution of marriage symbolizes the joining of two people and their families, so it is honored with special traditions.

African religious beliefs have a huge impact on the lives of their followers, both in everyday life and during their annual festivals. The Yoruba people honor deities such as Olodumare and Obatala, the two beings responsible for the creation of life on Earth, as well as other higher beings, during these ceremonies. After the Creator, the most important beings are the Orishas, who work as the intermediaries between mankind and the Supreme Being. Almost all the Orishas have several paths to them, and consequently, are responsible for giving different kinds of divination. The higher beings are all held in high esteem, whether it's because they can offer help or because they are feared due to their destructive nature.

Nowadays, this African belief system has had a significant influence - both on the life of its indigenous followers remaining in Africa and on the African diaspora living in various corners of the world. Fortunately, after centuries of misunderstandings and pressure from other religions, Yoruba devotees can now peacefully coexist among their neighbors with different religious beliefs and customs. While some Yoruba traditions changed and continue to evolve as a result of these circumstances, their true meaning has remained constant since the dawn of their civilization.

References

Adams, A. (2018, May 8). An introduction to Nigeria's Yoruba people. Retrieved from Theculturetrip.com website: https://the-culturetrip.com/africa/nigeria/articles/an-introduction-to-nigerias-yoruba-people/

Africa Update Archives. (n.d.). Retrieved from Ccsu.edu website: https://web.ccsu.edu/af-study/supdt99.htm

The Yoruba Religious concepts. (n.d.). Retrieved from Google.com website: https://sites.google.com/site/theyorubareligiousconcepts/home

Adams, A. (2018, May 8). An introduction to Nigeria's Yoruba people. Retrieved from Theculturetrip.com website: https://the-culturetrip.com/africa/nigeria/articles/an-introduction-to-nigerias-yoruba-people/

Aghadiuno, E. (n.d.). The Arts Under Colonial Administration. Retrieved from Onlinenigeria.com website: https://onlinenigeria.com/artsandcrafts/

b1005501 1. (n.d.). Retrieved from Oclc.org website: https://libmma.contentdm.oclc.org/digital/collection/p15324coll10/id/71017

Dúrójaiyé. (n.d.). Retrieved from Yorubaname.com website: https://www.yorubaname.com/entries/D%C3%BAr%C3%B3jaiy%C3%A9

Egu, K. C. (2011, March 16). Ile Ife, Nigeria (ca. 500 B.c.e.-). Retrieved from Blackpast.org website: https://www.blackpast.org/global-african-history/ile-ife-ca-500-b-c-e/

Konkwo, R. (2018, June 18). Yoruba Gods and Goddesses. Retrieved from Legit.ng website: https://www.legit.ng/1175618-yoruba-gods-goddesses.html

Law, R. (1984). How truly traditional is our traditional history? The case of Samuel Johnson and the recording of Yoruba oral tradition. History in Africa, 11, 195–221.

Newark Museum. (n.d.). Retrieved from Archive.org website: https://web.archive.org/web/20140810075351/http://newarkmuseum.org/museum_default_page.aspx?id=5080

No title. (n.d.). Retrieved from Unesco.org website: https://unesdoc.unesco.org/ark:/48223/pf0000042225

The Editors of Encyclopedia Britannica. (2019). Oyo empire. In Encyclopedia Britannica.

The Yoruba artist: new theoretical perspectives on African arts: Free Download, Borrow, and Streaming: Internet Archive. (n.d.). Retrieved from Archive.org website: https://archive.org/details/yorubaartistnewt0000unse

Yoruba. (n.d.). Retrieved from Everyculture.com website: https://www.everyculture.com/wc/Mauritania-to-Nigeria/Yoruba.html

YorubaNames. (n.d.). Retrieved from Yorubaname.com website: https://www.yorubaname.com/entries/M%C3%A1l%E1%BB%8Dm%E1%B-B%8D%CC%81

Sawe, B. E. (2019, April 17). What is the Yoruba religion? Yoruba beliefs and origin. Retrieved from Worldatlas.com website: https://www.worldatlas.com/articles/what-is-the-yoruba-religion.html

Wigington, P. (n.d.). Yoruba religion: History and beliefs. Retrieved from Learnreligions.com website: https://www.learnreligions.com/

Courlander, H. (1973). Tales of Yoruba gods and heroes. New York: Crown Publishers.

Africa Update Archives. (n.d.). Retrieved from Ccsu.edu website: https://web.ccsu.edu/af-study/supdt99.htm

artsconnectinternational. (2016, July 26). The Orishas — Arts Connect International. Retrieved from Artsconnectinternational.org website: https://www.artsconnectinternational.org/blog/index.php/2016/07/26/orishs

Dialogue Institute. (2020, September 16). Yoruba — Dialogue Institute. Retrieved from Dialogueinstitute.org website: https://dialogueinstitute.org/afrocaribbean-and-african-religion-information/2020/9/16/yoruba

Who are the Orishas? - DJONIBA Dance Center. (2016, September 20). Retrieved from Djoniba.com website: https://www.djoniba.com/who-are-the-orishas/

&amp, B. I. O., & Ifamena, I. (2020, April 25). Why is the Orisa Orunmila important in IFA tradition and culture? Retrieved from Ifaglobalsite.com website: https://www.ifaglobalsite.com/single-post/2020/04/25/what-is-orunmila-the-orisa-of-destiny-goal-for-humanity

Editors. (2021, June 8). Eleguá, Orisha of the Crossroads. Retrieved from Newyorklatinculture.com website: https://www.newyorklatinculture.com/elegua-orisha-of-the-crossroads/

Konkwo, R. (2018, June 18). Yoruba Gods and Goddesses. Retrieved from Legit.ng website: https://www.legit.ng/1175618-yoruba-gods-goddesses.html

magicalmaia, & View my complete profile. (n.d.). Magical Maia's Adventures. Retrieved from Blogspot.com website: http://magicalmaia.blogspot.com/2009/11/paths-of-yemaya.html

My Yoruba. (n.d.). Retrieved from Tumblr. com website: https://myoruba.tumblr.com/ post/87600370967/paths-of-elegua

Walker, S. (2021, April 27). The ancient beliefs of African goddesses. Retrieved from Amplifyafrica.org website: https://www.amplifyafrica.org/ post/the-ancient-beliefs-of-african-goddesses

Who are the Orishas? - DJONIBA Dance Center. (2016, September 20). Retrieved from Djoniba.com website: https://www.djoniba.com/ who-are-the-orishas/

YORUBA RELIGION: OSHUN. (n.d.). Retrieved from Blogspot.com website: https://cuban-yoruba.blogspot.com/2007/04/oshun.html

Burton, N. (2020, July 31). How some Black Americans are finding solace in African spirituality. Retrieved from Vox website: https://www.vox.com/2020/7/31/21346686/ orisha-yoruba-african-spirituality-covid

Google Arts & Culture. (n.d.). Yoruba people of West Africa. Retrieved from Google.com website: https://artsandculture.google.com/ usergallery/EQKyzgLnW1j4IQ

News. (n.d.). Retrieved from Ufl.edu website: https://news.clas.ufl.edu/the-survival-of-the-yoruba-healing-systems-in-the-modern-age/

Santería's impact cuts 2 ways – dollars & sense. (n.d.). Retrieved from Cuny.edu website: https://blogs.baruch.cuny.edu/dollarsand-sense/2016/06/27/concerns-mount-as-sante-rias-following-grows/

Siedlak, M. J. (2017). Seven African powers: The orishas. North Charleston, SC: Createspace Independent Publishing Platform.

Wigington, P. (n.d.). Yoruba religion: History and beliefs. Retrieved from Learnreligions.com website: https://www.learnreligions.com/yoruba-religion-4777660

Adams, A. (2018, May 8). An introduction to Nigeria's Yoruba people. Retrieved from Theculturetrip.com website: https://the-culturetrip.com/africa/nigeria/articles/an-introduction-to-nigerias-yoruba-people/

Printed in the USA
CPSIA information can be obtained
at www.ICGtesting.com
CBHW071319280824
13826CB00008B/45